We Love Baseball!

By Peggy Harrison

For Evan, my favorite baseball player

Thanks to Pat, Abigail and Cameron Scharf, Karen Ryan, Mary Michaela Murray, David Murray, Jim Waite and the McIntire Little League, Barbara Murray and Charlottesville T-ball, Blue Ridge Graphics, Downtown Athletics, Alana Magri, Richard, Ayla, and Mariah Palermo, Cliff Hayden, the parents, and all the baseball players: Olivia W. Allen, Garret and Ryan Brown, Amir Carter, Keith and Meg Cassells-Hamby, River Dale Frazier, Jacqueline Gunning, Elijah Haden, Evan Harrison-Bibb, Daniel Jones, Seyoun Kim, Charlie Murray, Bryan and Henry Pollard, Joshua and Zachary Scharf, Vivek Srivatsa, Marco Sun, Ravon Tinsley, Dixon and Katherine White, and Tré Wood.

A Random House PICTUREBACK® Book

Random House 🏠 New York

Hi, my name is Eli.
This spring, I'm
going to play on my
first real baseball
team!

Before the season starts, my dad helps me pick out my very own baseball glove. He tells me to pound the pocket with my fist to see how the glove fits. I try on *lots* of gloves, until I finally find one that's just my size!

Now I'm ready to PLAY BALL!

At our first practice, Coach Pat gives out jerseys with our team's name on them. We're called the **Smashers** because we're going to **smash** the ball way into the outfield!

———— batting helmet

Our coaches say it's important to always wear protective gear. Batters wear batting helmets to protect their heads.

catcher's mask

chest protector

leg guard

Catchers wear chest protectors, leg guards, and masks to keep them safe from flying balls and bats! Whoa! Who's that under all that gear?

It's my best friend, Josh! He's going to be our catcher.

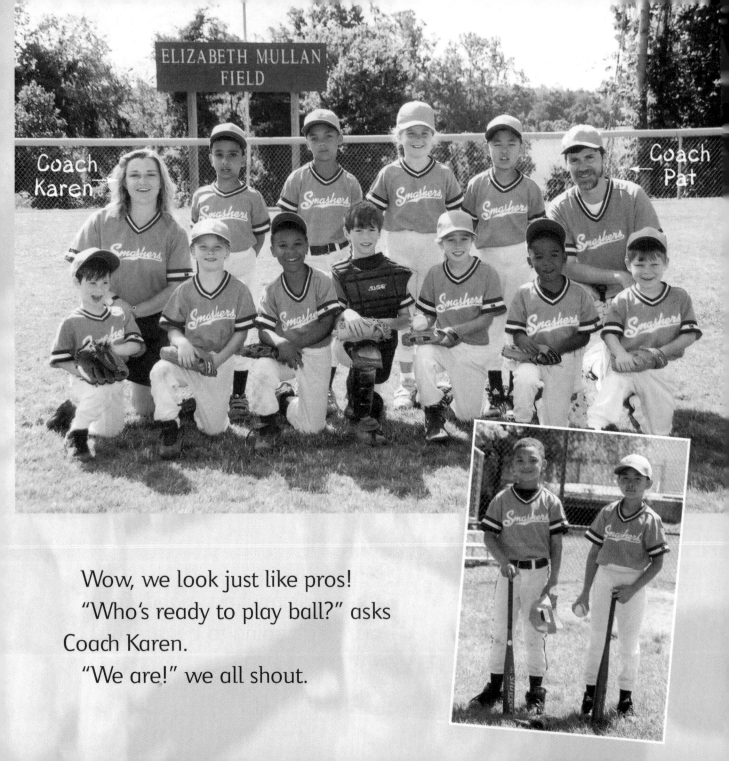

Wow, we look just like pros!
"Who's ready to play ball?" asks
Coach Karen.
"We are!" we all shout.

second base

third base

first base

pitcher's
mound

home plate

There's a lot to learn! Our coaches tell us the field we play on is called a baseball diamond. That's because the four bases make the shape of a diamond. Inside the diamond is called the infield. Outside the diamond is called the outfield.

We learn to catch different kinds of hits.

A **ground ball** is when the baseball comes bouncing along the ground. When we see a ground ball, we get in front of the ball, then bend down close to the ground to catch it.

"Use two hands!" says Coach Pat.

A **fly ball** is when the ball comes soaring through the air!

Oops!

Fly balls can be hard to catch.
Good try, Jacqueline!

My favorite part of practice is when we bat. When we're up, Coach Karen helps us find the right size bat—one that's not too heavy to swing!

Then she shows us how to grip the bat, one hand over the other. River's right-handed, so her right hand goes on top.

We wait for our turn on the bench.

If you swing at the ball and miss, it's called a strike. Three strikes and you're out! If you hit the ball and no one catches it, you can run to first base, or keep running until you get tagged out. Now it's Seyoun's turn to bat. He keeps his eye on the ball! He swings!

Crack! He hits the ball! Run the bases, Seyoun!

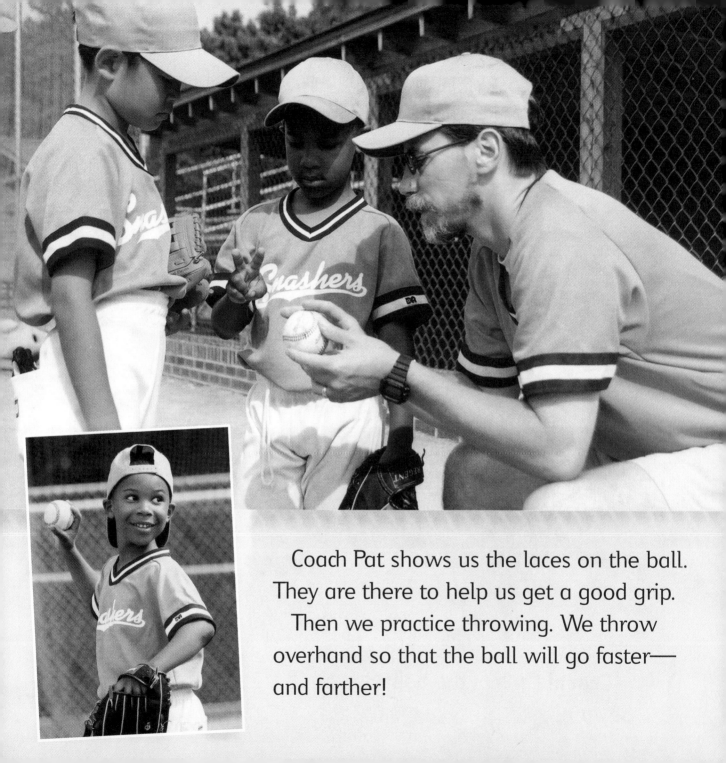

Coach Pat shows us the laces on the ball.
They are there to help us get a good grip.
Then we practice throwing. We throw
overhand so that the ball will go faster—
and farther!

With each practice, we learn to work together. By the end of practice, we're hot and dirty and ready for a cool break!

It's finally game day!
I see my dad sitting
right up front.

Coach Pat and Coach Karen give
us a pep talk in the dugout. "Go
out there and have fun!" they say.

We do a cheer before we head out. "Go, Smashers! Go, Smashers! Yeah!"

The team we're playing is called the **Bears**.
The first Bear steps up to the plate. **Grrrr!**

He pops the ball into the air! I'm playing shortstop, so I catch the ball and throw it back to the pitcher.

Amir, the center fielder, backs me up in case I miss.

Uh-oh! "The Zack Attack!" is up next. We've heard about him!
Whack! Zack hits the ball and takes off running.

He rounds first base, then second, then third! He slides into home! "Safe!" calls the umpire. Yikes! The Smashers need to get some runs, too!

All through the game we try our best.
Our coaches help us remember what to do.
When it's my turn to bat, I get a hit. Yes!

Then Meg slams a home run.

Our teammates give Meg
a high-five after she crosses
home plate!

GO, SMASHERS!

All our practice has paid off. After lots of hard playing, the Smashers win the game! Yeah!

We shake hands with the Bears to show that we're all still friends, no matter who won.

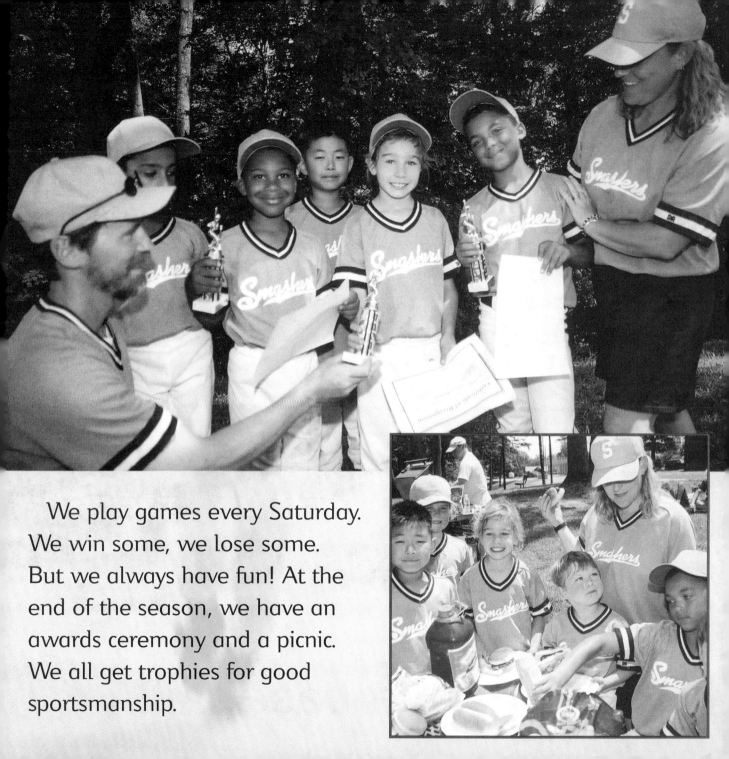

We play games every Saturday. We win some, we lose some. But we always have fun! At the end of the season, we have an awards ceremony and a picnic. We all get trophies for good sportsmanship.

This has been the best spring ever because
we love baseball!